IF THE GOLDEN HOUR WON'T COME FOR US
ADAMS ADEOSUN

For my mother, who shares a day with my country.

This is a work of fiction. All names, characters, places, and incidents are a product of the author's imagination. Any resemblance to real events or persons, living or dead, is entirely coincidental.

Published by Akashic Books
©2024 Adams Adeosun
ISBN: 978-1-63614-218-0

All rights reserved
Printed in China
First printing

Akashic Books
Instagram, X, Facebook: AkashicBooks
info@akashicbooks.com
www.akashicbooks.com

African Poetry Book Fund
Prairie Schooner
University of Nebraska
110 Andrews Hall
Lincoln, Nebraska 68588

TABLE OF CONTENTS

Preface by Mahtem Shiferraw 4

In the Beginning, Ablution 6
At the Altar 7
An Elegy for the Tenderhearted I 9
An Elegy for the Tenderhearted II 11
A House with a View 12
If the Golden Hour Won't Come for Us 14
A Door into Absence 16
I Too Have Known Despair 17
The Eye Is Not Satisfied with Seeing 19
Polygraph 21
A Triptych of Excuses for My Mother 23

PREFACE
by Mahtem Shiferraw

In the world of Adams Adeosun, the things unraveling aren't hiding behind shadows; there is nothing lurking beneath the lines, no one to be sought out and extracted or rescued. Settled in their discomfort, the speaker has allowed themself to trace their origin, their lineage, and their ancestry in a way that does not define nor contain them. At times, they become an animal softer than the body; at other times, they begin with their mother, "always home between a candle / and a keg of seawater." ("If the Golden Hour Won't Come for Us") Or they persist in their state of interrogation, which does not find them in the position of a supplicant, but rather one filled with a new kind of tenderness wielded in unexpected ways.

If there is anything to be traced in this wonderful collection, it is exactly that: the capacity of Adeosun to both surprise and surrender. Within the softness, there is self-determination and self-emancipation that could easily be missed; the speaker may be in a state of longing, but they are also their own liberator. They do not deny their struggles but instead choose to acknowledge them and leave them behind. And just when we think we have become acquainted with the speaker, they refuse to be contained. Instead they offer themself at the altar, both divine and not, miracle and not, rescuer of their own self, recognizing that "the journey is long and the body refuses the ark." ("At the Altar") This refusal allows them to make room for themself among other known and unknown divine bodies, as if to say, *this, too, is divine, can't you see it?* And we can, oh we can!

The refusal to be claimed is not done with arrogance nor does it stand out as an act of self-preservation; instead, it is a kindness that is bestowed upon the speaker by themself, and as a result, on the readers, those of us on the sidelines waiting to be rescued. This intentional mapping of multiple selves is almost surgical, done with such preciseness that, ultimately, we too will be embroiled in the metamorphosis that has been allowed to occur—so when they say, *in the beginning*, we begin with them too, coscripters of new origin stories, divinators of such golden hours.

If the Golden Hour Won't Come for Us is a superb collection. The poems' speakers refuse to be bound by their marred history but are still able to trace their lineage, filling themselves with light where once there may have been darkness. Here is where we can be both soft and strong, both witness and liberator, both joyful and homesick, where the definition of home continues to unravel throughout, each poem a new offering, a new land, a new divinity to unpeel and mark as our own. With this stunning new collection, Adeosun has given us new things we can marvel at and helped us look both inward and outward to unpathed ways, where our heads too can carry suns. ("The Eye Is Not Satisfied with Seeing")

IN THE BEGINNING, ABLUTION

And above all, I desire cleanness,
        baptism more than a scrubbing down,

an animal softer than my body
        bending me down under the skin of the sea,

blue sky lucid with revelation
        behind us, the dregs of my thirst

rippling out, my lungs bursting at the edge
        of myself, the glossolalia of my surrender

carried back to shore, more than a drowning,
        a return, salt to water, blood to the divine,

the baptizer, made holy by my filth, giving in
        to wings, the raptor of him slick with judgement.

Let me tell you now, everything looks perfect
        up above.

AT THE ALTAR
after Kaveh Akbar

I.

By now, I have traded gods once.
My mother, like the raven, molts.

We approach the church of the Cherubim
and the Seraphim on Eid ul-Fitr,

white sultana winging my body like I am
not sullied by Yâ-Sĩn, not ruined by An-Nās.

We are three at the altar—mother, son
and alóre. The congregation supplicate

to the Qibla today. By now, I have traded gods twice.
The world, like the puff adder, sheds snakeskin.

II.

Still, there must be use for me at the altar.
Not a giving to the knife as in Isaac,

not a leaving to the fire as in Abraham
before the angel, before the horned ram.

More than holiness, more than cleanness,
the Lord asking me for language,

the slow unravelling of Babel: *Read,*
in the name of your Lord who created man

from clinging clot.

III.

The sermon loses its way. Our alóre,
carpenter when time transcends breath, says,

Where there was a man, now there is a coffin.
The journey is long and the body refuses the ark;

yet, the mallet is master of the sea and master
of the clay. The clay caves, the ark exhales.

Auzubillah!

We are three at the altar, waiting anxiously
for a god who will claim us back but not like this.

AN ELEGY FOR THE TENDERHEARTED I

Oh, how sick, to fall in love with
the sweet saber of a canine racing

silently across the life of your wrist.
The light has gone out over the kitchen

table, the dead arm wrestling the clock,
floating up to its face with a pungent clarity,

waiting on the trickle of your blood,
for the sickle to cleave your bed.

Nothing kills a man
like what is in bed with him.

I owned a hound once, its coat too
black for brown, too brown for white;

or was it my mother's before me?
My mother, too woman for men,

too mother for her children, parting
the jaws of a dog to fill between its fangs

with love she can't put down. And me,
only when the dog was sick with love,

sick with death, its eyes rheumed black,
its coat colored by the earth, the spade

heavy in my hands, only then did it become mine.

AN ELEGY FOR THE TENDERHEARTED II

Not to be grim, but I am beginning
        to think there are no more stars

in the world, beginning to kill my darlings
        off the spare abacus of my toes, beginning

to feel the earth between my teeth.
        I'm interested in the ways a life

can be purchased. In this frame,
        I turn twenty-three keeping vigil over

my blood's blood in a ward.
        The puppeteer puts a boy in the next odd bed,

jumbled strings pulling him
        underwater, his lungs flowerpots

issuing humus, white carnation, and daytime
        nightmares. In the beginning,

                we agreed it was the end.

A HOUSE WITH A VIEW

Oh God, yes, I want a miracle
and a glass of wine to go with it.

A window for my mother, wide
and full, the girth of a kind world

in its watery eyes, a bouquet
of lights on the skin of the walls,

a Gerard roof, halfway house
for ospreys between river and sea—

a sign for my mother so she knows the wind
rustles my lungs even while I'm away—

and a yard in the back with wild Ixoras,
roosters, and no snakeskin. My mother

leaves the door open, and who can tell
what is coming before it rears its head?

My mother's father kept a bottle
of schnapps beside his bed,

green with miracle, a small offering
to whichever god came first, death

or my father's bone of contrition.
My father waited for death to arrive,

for the cleave of the sickle, the heave
of the body, the sigh of the soil,

the pressed loincloth of the newly ascended.
And even then, he waited for the bottle to dry.

My allegiance is fickle and I cannot hold
a grudge. I want all the fingers of rain

on my mother's roof and a glass of wine
in my left hand for whichever comes first,

the god of death or my father's bone
of contrition. Who can tell what is coming

before it rears its head? I want a house
for my mother, my father at the kitchen

table, the bottom of my glass damp
       with a miracle.

IF THE GOLDEN HOUR WON'T COME FOR US

I hope somewhere at the end of their journey, there is someone waiting for them, who calls them beloved.
—IfeOluwa Nihinlola

A curt nod, a furtive wave, a smile
across the aisle between the tamest of men

on a brokenhearted train in a brokenhearted
station, waiting to catch the golden hour

of the sun, like an outside cat on a semi-
detached fence, like an agama laundering

its own crown. The platform is empty.
The platform is desert concrete over a secret history.

The platform is as brokenhearted as the tannest
of men. The golden hour comes for the camera,

not the brokenhearted eye. The cat is black
and the agama is a monarchy of ugly.

The golden hour—no, *the spiteful sun*—
gives me to déjà vu, mental turbulence and

a terrible itch. I light a small fire to see before me.
Another, a tribute to the brotherhood of the aisle.

My mother is always home between a candle
and a keg of seawater. Your father is everywhere

but where the fire needs tending. The problem
is I sleep better in a stranger's bed, not at all

in mine. The problem is melatonin chucks me
to sleep paralysis and night terrors.

Once, after the golden hour eluded me yet again,
I dreamed I died and crows took my eyes

for their chicks, vultures carried my flesh
across the sunrise. My mother named me

for a soft place to land. I'm sorry I'm not
filled with hope like a good citizen.

If the golden hour won't come for us,
can I come home with you for the night?

A DOOR INTO ABSENCE

In the near future, a revolving door,
a carousel, an Echolac bag black with absence,

seams stretched by a one-way loneliness,
weighted inside with jars emptied of strawberry

jam and crammed full with the grainy salt
of memory, all the wuthering promises

of a departure lounge. For now, the hearth
of a candle, two die in a white cup and home

split in four on a Ludo board between
my mother and me. She tosses the die,

a dot and a dot staring back at us
like the wet eyes of some soft-skulled animal.

My mother, full of divination, full of signs
and symbols, says to leave a child behind

when I go away, and I lose myself in a cry-laugh.
I say I'm almost too son for offspring, *Mother;*

I say I'm almost too home for exile.
My Echolac, already weary at the zips, sighs

      out of the sewing machine.

I TOO HAVE KNOWN DESPAIR

Struck by the great disease of loneliness,
I do nothing but lie in bed at night,

I do nothing but count back to my nothing,
wondering if my moon, sick with the terror

of the sun, is the same as my mother's.
My first memory of my mother, a broken tooth.

The second, my fingers a fine-tooth
comb at the back of her head.

She won't let me forget we were both born
on a Friday. Instead of a son, I have grown

into a diagnosis, every sea I cross running
back to my mother's feet, the sharp sand

of my sins cutting between her tender toes.
On my last night in her light, my mother

tried to teach me how to love:

> *If the wild heart of your eyes happens to fall on*
> *a soft animal, a false rib holy as the first horse,*
>
> *give it a toothbrush, a fine-tooth comb or*
> *a ribbon to keep the falling out of its face.*

Things the living can use or keep under a pillow.
Flowers are for the sickbed and the deathbed

and all the other beds in want of color
on the roadside to your bone-white lonely.

But, Mother, my beloved gives me nothing but flowers.
The war is never lost nor won; only time hurtles

forward, eager for the son to become the father.
I have no inheritance but my father's absence.

THE EYE IS NOT SATISFIED WITH SEEING

This old lady, she stopped me. She said, "Runnin' around, catching up all that light. In moonlight, black boys look blue. You blue, that's what I'm gon' call you. 'Blue'."
—*Moonlight*, written/directed by Barry Jenkins

I am black in every light except
for black, in which I am blue

before the mirror, in which I am
cornflower cold in your palms.

In the grove of my name,
water files a rock clean.

Miracles are often more silent
than the faithful confess.

What does it mean that my beloved
has all the language for blue?

Aqua, azure, bice, Capri, cerulean,
cyan, Egyptian, electric, gunmetal.

The sea is sharp on both sides and
sometimes a thing is spoiled

by the clangor of its name.
Are you listening? Are you listening?

Horizon, indigo, iris, light, Marian,
midnight, Majorelle, reflex, robin egg.

What does it mean that my beloved
finds an omen in the blue of a robin's egg?

In every painting of an eagle,
the end of days is behind.

All the wonder in the world leads
me back to my mother's embrace.

Sapphire, sky, steel, teal, tekhelet,
true, turquoise, ultramarine, viridian, zaffer.

Wandering in a museum, a basket of sun
on my head, I come to a horse painted

blue with seawater and think it
        a sacrificial billy.

POLYGRAPH
We are liars and cowards all, or nearly all, or nearly all the time.
—James Baldwin

On the comedown, schooling
my mouth to be honest again,

I say I'm whole, I say I'm holy,
I say I'm a new animal at home
        in the sun.

My heart hums and hums like a mockingbird,
its music sinking to my belly, silent
        where it is a prayer.

Loath to find that I'm who I've always been,
I conjure my father's head for comfort.

My father, haloed with judgement, finds
two punishable offenses in my image:

        One,
            you are under high-tension electric wires.
        Two,
            you have plaited your hair like a woman,
                any reason?

Silently as tomorrow, I give up
my father's likeness for my mother's.

I'm glad you're happy, my mother's head sings,

blind to my high-tension electric wires,

> *but you should know that*
> *the love is gone from the pantry,*
>
> *my stove is still damp*
> *with the amniotic fluid of your birth,*
>
> *and my account is empty,*
> *whichever way you look at it;*
>
> *in the meantime, can I hold on*
> *to some of your happiness?*

I say I'm homesick for the knife
and homesick for the fire.

I say after family, the devil
is God's greatest invention.

The mockingbird stills in my chest,
dizzy with the weight of truth.

A TRIPTYCH OF EXCUSES FOR MY MOTHER

I.

Mother, time has turned out
to be an illusion and my clock

is always six hours behind my heart
and what is past hurtles ahead of me

and the night comes too early
or too late and I swear the cold

is always in my blood and tomorrow
is deferred until December

and what do you mean *happy new month?*

II.

Mother, my voice is a hummingbird
hovering somewhere between

Murtala Muhammed and Orchard Field
and there is nothing baggage claim

can do for me and what is lost
quietly approaches what is dead

and I have given up dreams of the choir
and what can I say to *no evil agenda shall come*

to pass in Jesus's name but a reluctant
              amen?

III.

And, Mother, the coast is too far for baptism
and I'm a litany of especially heinous sins

and I have taken my body back from the altar
and filled it with New Amsterdam, Marlboro,

and cunnilingus and I can't go to sleep without
these drugs and you can't save me from these men

and, Mother, language has gone from between us.